Step-by-Step
Stories

A+
books

Recycling, Step by Step

by Jean M. Lundquist

A+ Books are published by Capstone Press,
151 Good Counsel Drive, P.O. Box 669, Mankato, Minnesota 56002.
www.capstonepub.com

 Books published by Capstone Press are manufactured with paper
containing at least 10 percent post-consumer waste.

Library of Congress Cataloging-in-Publication Data
Lundquist, Jean (Jean M.)
  Recycling, step by step / by Jean Lundquist.
    p. cm.—(A+ books. Step-by-step stories)
  ISBN 978-1-4296-6026-6 (library binding)
  1. Recycling (Waste, etc.)—Juvenile literature. I. Title.

TD794.5.L86 2012
363.72'82—dc22

2011002616

Credits

Shelly Lyons, editor; Ted Williams, designer; Marcie Spence, media researcher; Sarah Schuette, photo stylist;
  Marcy Morin, studio scheduler; Eric Manske, production specialist

Photo Credits

Alamy Images: Aurora Photos, 22, Chris Selby, 19 (left), Mikhail Kondrashov "fotmik", 15 (right), Phil Degginger,
cover (middle), Pierre Brye, 15 (left), Visions of America LLC, 14; AP Images: Al Behrman, 19 (right); Capstone
Studio: Karon Dubke, cover (left), 1, 4-5, 8, 9, 10 (inset), 13, 14 (inset), 17 (bottom), 18 (left), 20-21, 22 (inset),
25, 26-27, 28 (right), 29 (left); Corbis: Bob Krist, 10-11, 28 (left); Dreamstime: Willyvend, 23; Landov: Andreas
Lander/DPA, 16, Brian Snyder/Reuters, 12, 29 (right), Franz-Peter Tschauner/DPA, 18 (right), 18-19, Patrick Pleul/
DPA, 16 (inset); Nigel Dickinson, 24; Shutterstock: alterfalter, 12 (inset), andrej pol, 17 (top), Dmitriy Shironosov, 7
(bottom left), Morgan Lane Photography, 7 (top), rezachka, cover (right), 7 (bottom right), s_oleg, design element,
vladislav_studio, 6

Note to Parents, Teachers, and Librarians

Step-by-Step Stories is a nonfiction set that teaches sequencing skills along with solid information about the title
subjects. Through fun text and photos, this set supports math and science concepts such as order of events,
relative position words, and ordinal positions. Use the exercise on page 28 to help children practice their
sequencing skills.

Printed in the United States of America in North Mankato, Minnesota.
032011   006110CGF11

Table of Contents

1

What Is Recycling?

Do you recycle? Like many people in the United States, Erica recycles every day. Each week, Erica carries her family's full recycling bin to the curb.

Many items can be recycled. Plastic, steel, glass, and cardboard are just a few. Look around your home. What can you recycle?

Erica knows when things are recycled they change form. Then they are made into something new. But *how* are things recycled?

5

There are three main steps in recycling:

The recycling symbol is called the "chasing arrows." It stands for the three steps in recycling. Gary Anderson created the symbol in 1970.

6

In the first step, the items are collected.

In the second step, they are cleaned and formed into something new.

In the third step, the new item is put on a store shelf for someone to buy.

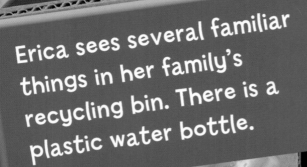

Erica sees several familiar things in her family's recycling bin. There is a plastic water bottle.

A glass pickle jar is in the bin.

The steel can that held Erica's peas is in here too.

This is the cardboard box that held Erica's birthday gift from her grandma.

A truck comes to the curb to pick up Erica's bin. The truck collects recycling from other houses too. This is the first step in recycling.

2

Plastic Bottles

Now, let's follow the plastic bottle's journey.

After the truck picks up the bottle, it goes to a plastics recycling plant. All of the bottles there are sorted by the numbers they have on them. Erica's bottle has the word "PETE" and the number "1" on it.

More PETE bottles are recycled in the United States than any other type of plastic. Soft drinks and peanut butter are often packaged in PETE bottles or jars.

At the plant, the PETE bottles begin the second step of recycling. They are ground up until they are flakes. Then the flakes are washed and dried.

Next the flakes are melted. Then the plastic can be molded into something new.

In the third step of recycling, the new item is placed on a store shelf. Erica could pick up the new bottle of water at the store!

The melted plastic can be made into carpet, clothing, or even the fuzz on a tennis ball. Often it is made into a brand new bottle.

13

3

Steel

In the first step of recycling Erica's steel can, the can is taken to a collection area. Once there, the small amount of tin is removed.

SANITATION
36585

Next the cans are pressed into large bales or bricks.

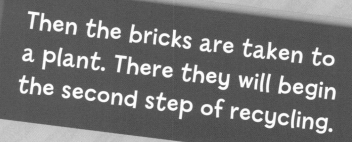

Then the bricks are taken to a plant. There they will begin the second step of recycling.

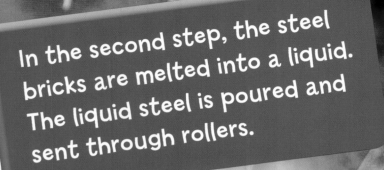

In the second step, the steel bricks are melted into a liquid. The liquid steel is poured and sent through rollers.

The rollers flatten the steel into sheets. Then the steel can become something new.

In the third step, another person uses the steel item. Erica imagines the can that once held peas sailing on the ocean as part of a ship. The can may also return as another can.

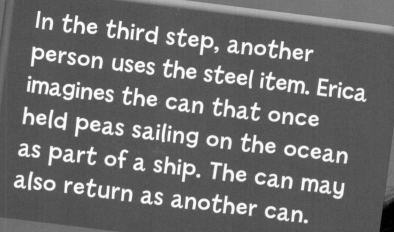

Steel is recycled more than any other material in the world. In fact, new steel can't be made without recycled steel.

4

Glass

What about the glass jar in Erica's bin? In the first step of recycling, the truck sends the jar to a glass recycling plant.

In the second step, the glass containers are sorted by color. The colors of glass are clear, green, blue, and brown.

Next the glass is crushed into small pieces called cullet. The cullet is melted into a liquid.

The liquid glass is measured into the right amount to make a new glass container. This amount is called a "gob of glass."

Within 30 days, the whole process can be completed. The third step in recycling happens when Erica's family picks up the new pickle jar at the store. Can you think of other things that come in glass jars?

If you recycle one glass bottle, the amount of energy saved could power a 100-watt light bulb for four hours!

5

Cardboard and Paper

In the first step of recycling Erica's cardboard box, the truck takes the cardboard to a collection center.

There workers flatten and bind all the cardboard into bales. Then the bales are taken to a paper mill.

At the paper mill, the cardboard begins the second step of recycling. It is mixed with water and swished around. The mixture of cardboard and water is called slurry. In this step, ink is washed out of the cardboard.

Soon the slurry is sprayed onto a screen. The slurry then runs through rollers to press out more water. After the screen takes a trip through a big oven called a dryer, most of the water is gone. Only paper is left.

In the second step of recycling, the paper is made into new cardboard. In the third step, the new cardboard box will hold a gift from Erica to her grandmother.

Erica now knows what happens to her plastic bottles, steel cans, glass jars, and cardboard boxes.

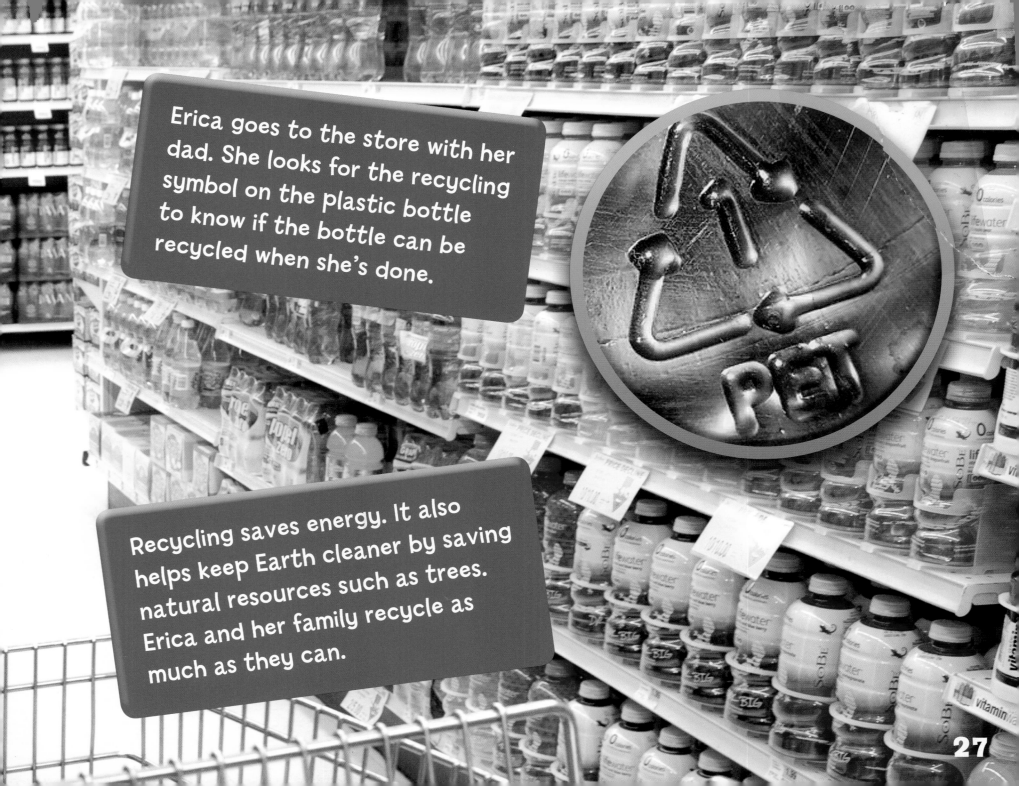

Erica goes to the store with her dad. She looks for the recycling symbol on the plastic bottle to know if the bottle can be recycled when she's done.

Recycling saves energy. It also helps keep Earth cleaner by saving natural resources such as trees. Erica and her family recycle as much as they can.

27

Mixed-up Mess!

Now that you've learned all about recycling, can you put these steps for recycling a plastic bottle in order?

A The bottles are sorted.

B A truck collects the bottles.

C The bottles are melted and made into something new.

D The bottles are ground into flakes.

Glossary

bale—a large bundle tied tightly together

cullet—crushed glass ready to be recycled

flake—a small piece of plastic created when plastic bottles are ground up for recycling

gob of glass—the amount of liquid glass needed to make a new glass jar or bottle

mold—to form something

natural resource—a material from nature, such as oil or trees, that is useful to people

recycle—to make used items into new products

slurry—the mixture of cardboard and water created when cardboard is recycled

Read More

Internet Sites

Johnson, J. Angelique. *The Eco-Family's Guide to Living Green.* Point It Out! Tips for Green Living. Mankato, Minn.: Picture Window Books, 2011.

Mackenzie, Anne L. *Let's Recycle!* Caring for the Earth. Mankato, Minn.: Capstone Press, 2007.

Minden, Cecilia. *Kids Can Reuse.* 21st Century Basic Skills Library. Ann Arbor, Mich.: Cherry Lake Pub., 2010.

FactHound offers a safe, fun way to find Internet sites related to this book. All of the sites on FactHound have been researched by our staff.

Here's all you do:

Visit *www.facthound.com*

Type in this code: 9781429660266

Super-cool stuff!

Check out projects, games and lots more at **www.capstonekids.com**

31

Index